SHARON ROBINSON

PROMISES TO KEEP

HOW JACKIE ROBINSON CHANGED AMERICA

SCHOLASTIC INC.
New York Toronto London Auckland Sydney
Mexico City New Delhi Hong Kong Buenos Aires

ISBN 0-439-67875-7

12 11 10 9 8 7 6 5 4 3 2 5 6 7 8 9 10/0

Printed in the U.S.A. 66

First Scholastic paperback printing, February 2005

The text type was set in 13-point Perpetua.
Book design by Kristina Albertson

PHOTO CREDITS

INTERIOR: ALL PHOTOGRAPHS ARE COURTESY OF THE ROBINSON FAMILY AND THE JACKIE ROBINSON FOUNDATION UNLESS NOTED BELOW: 3: NATIONAL BASEBALL HALL OF FAME LIBRARY, COOPERSTOWN, NY; 4 (LEFT): CORBIS; 4 (RIGHT): AP/WIDE WORLD PHOTOS; 5 (LEFT): ZINDMAN/FREMONT; 5 (RIGHT): CORBIS; 8: COLLECTION OF THE NEW YORK HISTORICAL SOCIETY; 9: REPRODUCED FROM THE COLLECTIONS OF THE LIBRARY OF CONGRESS; 10 (TOP): TK; 10 (BOTTOM): BETTMANN/CORBIS; 11 (BOTH): NEW YORK PUBLIC LIBRARY, SCHOMBURG CENTER FOR BLACK STUDIES; 14 (LEFT TOP TO BOTTOM): UNIVERSITY OF CHICAGO, SPECIAL COLLECTIONS; NEW YORK PUBLIC LIBRARY; LIBRARY OF CONGRESS; 14 (RIGHT): AP/WIDE WORLD PHOTOS; 15 (LEFT): BETTMANN/CORBIS; 15 (RIGHT TOP TO BOTTOM): ALFREDO VALENTE/SCHOLASTIC PHOTO ARCHIVE; GORDON PARKS/LIBRARY OF CONGRESS [LC-USLV3-3384-1]; THE ESTATE OF CARL VAN VECHTEN. JOSEPH SOLOMON EXECUTOR/SCHOLASTIC PHOTO ARCHIVE; 17: NEW YORK PUBLIC LIBRARY, SCHOMBURG CENTER FOR BLACK STUDIES; 18: AP/WIDE WORLD PHOTOS; 19 (RIGHT): AP/WIDE WORLD PHOTOS; 20 (BOTTOM): NEW YORK PUBLIC LIBRARY, SCHOMBURG CENTER FOR BLACK STUDIES; 21 (TOP): U.S. ARMY NEWS FEATURES; 23: AP/WIDE WORLD PHOTOS; 24–25: NATIONAL BASEBALL HALL OF FAME LIBRARY, COOPERSTOWN, NY; 26: NATIONAL BASEBALL HALL OF FAME LIBRARY, COOPERSTOWN, NY; 27: PAGE FROM *LOOK* MAGAZINE/LIBRARY OF CONGRESS; 29 (BOTTOM): AP/WIDE WORLD PHOTOS; 30: E. E. JOSEPH STUDIOS/ROBINSON FAMILY COLLECTION; 31 (TOP): ZINDMAN/FREMONT, COURTESY OF THE AUTHOR; 31 (BOTTOM): CHARLES FEENEY PHOTOS, COURTESY OF THE AUTHOR; 32: LOGO REPRODUCED WITH PERMISSION FROM THE HILTON CINCINNATI NETHERLAND PLAZA; 33: AP/WIDE WORLD PHOTOS; 34: BETTMANN/CORBIS; 35: AP/WIDE WORLD PHOTOS; 36 (TOP): INTERNATIONAL NEWS PHOTO COURTESY OF THE AUTHOR; 36 (BOTTOM): JOHN DOMINIS/TIME LIFE PICTURES/GETTY IMAGES; 37: CORBIS; 38: AP/WIDE WORLD PHOTOS; 39: MAJOR LEAGUE BASEBALL TRADEMARKS AND COPYRIGHTS ARE USED WITH PERMISSION OF MAJOR LEAGUE BASEBALL PROPERTIES, INC.; 40: PHILIP SCHULTZ/TEX-JINX PRODUCTIONS, COURTESY OF THE AUTHOR; 41: NATIONAL BASEBALL HALL OF FAME LIBRARY, COOPERSTOWN, NY; 43 (LEFT): BETTMANN/CORBIS; 43 (RIGHT): AP/WIDE WORLD PHOTOS; 45 (RIGHT): J. R. EYERMAN/COURTESY OF THE AUTHOR; 47: ARTHUR ROTHSTEIN/*LOOK* MAGAZINE COLLECTION/LIBRARY OF CONGRESS; 48: BETTMANN/CORBIS; 49: NATIONAL BASEBALL HALL OF FAME LIBRARY, COOPERSTOWN, NY; 50: *LOOK* MAGAZINE COLLECTION/LIBRARY OF CONGRESS; 52 (BOTTOM): CORBIS; 53 (TOP RIGHT): AP/WIDE WORLD PHOTOS; 54 (LEFT): BETTMANN/CORBIS; 55 (LEFT): BETTMANN/CORBIS; 56: AP/WIDE WORLD PHOTOS; 57 (TOP): AFP VIA GETTY IMAGES; 57 (BOTTOM): PETER SIMON; 58: *MINNEAPOLIS STAR TRIBUNE*, COURTESY OF THE NATIONAL BASEBALL HALL OF FAME LIBRARY, COOPERSTOWN, NY; 59: MAJOR LEAGUE BASEBALL; 60–61: ALLEN MORGAN FOR THE JACKIE ROBINSON FOUNDATION; 62: JOHN VECCIOLA.

JACK ROOSEVELT ROBINSON

BROOKLYN N.L. 1947 TO 1956

LEADING N.L. BATTER IN 1949. HOLDS FIELDING MARK FOR SECOND BASEMAN PLAYING IN 150 OR MORE GAMES WITH .992. LED N.L. IN STOLEN BASES IN 1947 AND 1949. MOST VALUABLE PLAYER IN 1949. LIFETIME BATTING AVERAGE .311. JOINT RECORD HOLDER FOR MOST DOUBLE PLAYS BY SECOND BASEMAN, 137 IN 1951. LED SECOND BASEMEN IN DOUBLE PLAYS 1949-50-51-52.

Jackie Robinson's plaque from the Baseball Hall of Fame

In memory of my beloved brother, Jack Roosevelt Robinson, Jr.

—S.R.

ACKNOWLEDGMENTS

Let me begin by giving thanks to my mother, Rachel Robinson, for her love, generosity, and belief in this project. Much love and thanks to my son, Jesse Simms, and my brother, David. I'd like to thank the entire Scholastic family, but most especially Dick Robinson, Barbara Marcus, Jean Feiwel, Steve Palm, Shelley White, Judy Newman, and Charisse Meloto. A very special thank-you to my editor, Sheila Keenan, and to art director Kristina Albertson. I'd also like to thank all my coworkers at Major League Baseball with special thanks to Commissioner Bud Selig and MLB President Bob DuPuy. I'd like to thank Jana Perry, Kimberly Allen-King, and Mariner Brito for their friendship, support, and assistance with photo research. Special thanks to Leonard Coleman, Marty and Nancy Edelman, Carole Coleman, Brenda Miller, Janus Adams, Jim Kelly, Robyn Liverant, Vargrave Richards, Emma Sun, Debbie Sun, Carol Grant, Wendy Lewis, Raymond Scott, Marcia Rubenstein, KC Wilson, Nel Yomtov, Donna Christianson and John Blundell. I love each of you.

Deep gratitude to the Jackie Robinson Foundation, the Library of Congress, and the Baseball Hall of Fame for giving me access to their incredible collections.

Contents

Introduction

On April 15, 1947, my father, Jack Roosevelt Robinson, stepped out of the Brooklyn Dodgers dugout, crossed first base, and assumed his position as first baseman. He paused, hands resting on bent knees, toes pointed in, then stood, lifted his cap, and saluted the cheering fans. It was a defining moment for baseball—and for America.

As a result of Dad's accomplishments on and off the field, I inherited a legacy of excellence and service. Today this legacy takes me into classrooms across the United States, Canada, and the Caribbean. As the Vice President of Educational Programming for Major League Baseball, I bring the *Breaking Barriers* program into schools, where children, ballplayers, and I talk baseball, values, and books. The kids are naturally curious about my childhood. They want to know what was it like being Jackie Robinson's daughter.

They ask me questions such as, "Did your dad come home angry after losing a baseball game?" or, "How did you and your family feel about the hate letters you got?" But the question that makes me stop and think hardest has been, "Did you *really* know your father?"

When kids ask me that question, I tell them I was six when my dad retired from baseball; twelve when he was elected into the Hall of Fame; twenty-two when he died. I also tell the children that my father taught me to flip pancakes, hit a baseball, question political leaders, solve problems, and keep promises.

Whether I was learning to walk, wildly swinging the bat at a fastball, tackling one of my brothers during a football game, or singing a show tune from *West Side Story* on the rock ledge of our fireplace, Dad encouraged me with his praise and loving smile. At times, my father made me feel like I was the most important person in his life. He was fond of saying, "Just put your fingertip in my tea and I won't need any sugar." I'd giggle and believe I actually had the power to sweeten that cup! When I was sad, Dad was there for me. The first time I cried over failed love, he sat on my bed and reminded me that I deserved better.

Over the years, I've learned about my father's baseball days from friends, family, other ballplayers, and even strangers who are anxious to share cherished Jackie Robinson memories with me. To this day, I'm mesmerized by newsreels of my dad rounding the bases, joyously clapping his hands as he outfoxes another pitcher.

My father was famous. My brothers and I grew up among awards, trophies, and photographs, but our parents taught us not to worship these honors. They said we should measure our lives by the impact we had on other people's lives. All we had to do was pay attention to the way our parents lived to know that this was true.

As a kid, my favorite photograph hung on the wall leading to the lower level of our house. It showed my dad stealing home plate during the 1955 World Series. I passed it several times a day and always paused to look at how a cloud of dirt obscured half my dad's body, or to study the way his right hand was clenched into a fist. I never failed to notice how my dad's face twisted with fierce determination. Could this be the same man who never raised his voice at home?

Looking back I realize that one of the things I admired most about my father was how he stayed in the game until the end. He stood firm even when his opinion wasn't popular. Whether questioning an umpire or an American president, Dad used his celebrity to challenge an unjust system and support a movement organized to correct the wrongs.

So, yes, I knew my dad well as a father and as a man.

This brings me to why I wrote *Promises to Keep*. Though my father's story has been told many times, I wanted the opportunity to tell it in its fullness. *Promises to Keep* is more than a photographic biography. It's a story about commitment. I've chronicled my father's life through words and pictures as a lasting memory to a man who was shaped by American history and who had an impact on American history. As you read *Promises to Keep,* you'll see that my father's personal and professional experiences, like baseball itself, reflected the American experience of his time.

A lifetime of service was my father's commitment to America and his challenge to you. Whether you commit to study hard, to be a better friend, family member, or neighbor, I hope that through my father's example you will understand why making a promise and keeping it is so important.

—S. R.

My Dad and me

A Black and White World

My great-grandparents were slaves; my grandmother was a sharecropper; my father was born into a segregated world. Although it may be hard for you to imagine an America where black and white people were kept apart by laws and customs, that world existed.

My father helped change it.

By breaking the color barrier in Major League Baseball, my father helped break down racial segregation. Before we get into the story of Jackie Robinson, however, we need to understand how segregation became a way of life in the United States.

Slave quarters, c. 1860-63

The story of race relations in the United States begins more than 400 years ago, when African men, women, and children were enslaved and forcibly brought to the American colonies. The Civil War (1861–65) ended this terrible, inhumane practice. By 1870, there were approximately 4,000,000 African Americans in the United States who, because of the Thirteenth and Fourteenth Amendments to the Constitution, were now U.S. citizens.

As freedmen and women, some former slaves attended school for the first time, farmed in a system called sharecropping, voted, and held local, state, and federal offices. But the new

1619
People kidnapped from Africa are brought to the Virginia colony.

1776
There are approximately 2 million slaves in the American colonies. After the American Revolution (1775–1783), approximately 55,000 free black people live in what is now the United States.

1787
The U.S. Constitution does not mention slavery, but it does ban the importation of slaves as of 1808.

1861–65
The Civil War rages between the Union (the North) and the Confederacy (the South).

freedoms granted to African Americans were unacceptable to many southern whites who were used to being in control. These southerners used political, legal, and violent means to control blacks. They passed state laws to restrict the rights of blacks and to keep them from voting. Even the courts denied blacks opportunities and basic human rights. In *Plessy* v. *Ferguson* (1896), the U.S. Supreme Court upheld a state's right to pass racial segregation laws. The Supreme Court's ruling said that such laws did not violate the U.S. Constitution.

The nation was divided: those favoring segregation against those who opposed it.

The period of legal segregation in America is commonly referred to as the Jim Crow era. In the 1830s, Thomas Rice, a famous white music-hall entertainer in Baltimore, Maryland, created a fictional character based on a black singer-dancer. Rice called his character "Jim Crow." White audiences laughed at the clowning and foolish antics of the character. Black people found the performances demeaning. They began to use the term "Jim Crow" to mean discrimination.

This nineteenth-century sheet music shows a Jim Crow figure. Notice that the song is sung by T. (Thomas) Rice in "Ethiopian." Ethiopia is a country in Africa.

1863
President Abraham Lincoln signs the Emancipation Proclamation, which frees slaves in the Confederate states.

1865
The Thirteenth Amendment to the Constitution makes slavery illegal everywhere in the United States.

1868
The Fourteenth Amendment guarantees all people born in the United States, including African Americans, citizenship and equal protection under the law. Native Americans are not included.

1870
The Fifteenth Amendment grants all adult male citizens the right to vote.

Signs of Hope

Many public places, especially in the South, were segregated.

In the post–Civil War segregated world, black people and white people went to separate schools, ate in separate restaurants, stayed in separate hotels, and sat in different sections on trains and buses. In many places, they used different bathrooms, telephone booths, and water fountains. Blacks and whites went to separate pool halls, auditoriums, and circuses. Many blacks were restricted from using parks, libraries, and hospitals that served white people. Signs on public facilities often read COLORED and WHITE in an effort to keep one race from coming in contact with the other. Segregation was part of everyday life almost everywhere, especially in the South.

My father was six months old in the summer of 1919, the "Red Summer." African-American blood flowed as black people were assaulted and killed in race riots and lynchings. The racial tension escalated when southern blacks moved north to work in jobs created by World War I. From 1915 to 1930, nearly 1.5 million

Signs of the times: People were even prohibited from drinking at the same fountain.

black people migrated north at a rate of 100,000 per year. Many of them settled in New York, Chicago, St. Louis, and Detroit.

The black families who fled the South during this period hoped to find a better life and escape Jim Crow life. However, they soon discovered that Jim Crow traveled, too. The rapid shift in population caused overcrowding in many cities and increased resentment from many white workers who were now forced to work alongside blacks.

When African-American families left the South, they took with them their hopes for freedom and opportunity.

Mallie Robinson, my grandmother, was one of the early, pioneering migrants. She lived on a farm in Cairo, Georgia, in 1919, with her husband, Jerry, and their five children. They were sharecroppers, which meant they farmed a section of land owned by whites for a share of the profit from the crops. This system kept black sharecroppers like my grandparents from getting ahead. Sharecroppers didn't own their own farms. They had to buy all their seeds, food, and equipment on credit from the white landowner. At the end of the year, the black farmer had to give the white landowner up to one-half of his crop and repay all the credit. The black farmers ended up with very little and often owed money to the white owner.

Mallie Robinson and her five children, from left to right: Mack, my dad, Edgar, Willa Mae, Frank. They moved from Georgia to California in the early 1920s.

After dealing with the frustrations of sharecropping, Jerry Robinson gave up and deserted the family. Mallie couldn't maintain the farm on her own. But my grandmother was a determined woman with an unflappable faith in God. She packed up her children—Frank, Mack, Edgar, Willa Mae, and Jackie—and took a huge risk. Mallie and her family left the only life they'd ever known. They traveled by train to Pasadena, California. There, they lived with her brother until Mallie found work and a place for her family to live.

My grandmother worked long hours cleaning and cooking in the homes of white families. Meanwhile, she insisted her children keep up their grades, work after school, and attend church every Sunday. The children learned early to protect each other. For a couple of years my dad's sister, Willa Mae, took my father to school with her. Dad played alone in a sandbox outside her classroom until the kids came out for recess.

As a boy, Dad went to Cleveland and Washington Elementary schools in Pasadena. The students were black. The teachers were white. My father only got average grades, but he loved sports. With marbles, soccer, dodge ball, and baseball, Dad's reputation as a competitor—and a winner—began when he was just a young boy.

Pasadena was a pretty city with lots of parks and other public recreational facilities. My dad couldn't go in most of them. The local YMCA refused my father membership because he was black. The Pasadena movie houses he went to forced black people to sit in one section. The local soda fountain wouldn't serve black kids. Pasadena was divided into neighborhoods according to race. The boundaries were clearly drawn. Blacks lived in only certain parts of town. That didn't stop my grandmother.

Mallie and her sister and brother-in-law, Cora and Samuel Wade, raised enough money to buy a house. They ignored the racial boundaries and settled on a house at 121 Pepper Street. The house that they wanted happened to be in an all-white neighborhood. According to family stories, my grandmother knew that the owners wouldn't sell their home to a black family. Mallie got a light-skinned niece, who could pass for white, to purchase the Pepper Street house for them. After the closing, the Robinson and Wade families moved in together. The neighbors weren't exactly welcoming.

Mallie Robinson watches Jackie Robinson play ball with his nephews in the yard of the house at 121 Pepper Street. My father lived in the house until 1941.

My father was three years old when he and his family moved to Pepper Street. When he was eight, Dad got into a name-calling fight with the little white girl who lived across the street. The children's verbal battle was interrupted when the girl's father came outside and started throwing rocks at my father. There were other incidents like that meant to intimidate my grandmother into moving off Pepper Street. A cross was burned on their front lawn. But in spite of the pressure from neighbors, my grandmother refused to leave Pepper Street. Over time, the block became mixed with families from black, white, Asian, and Hispanic backgrounds.

Mississippi-born journalist Ida B. Wells (1862–1931) used the media to expose the violence African Americans were often subjected to in the 1890s and early 20th century. Wells researched and documented the shocking number of lynchings of black people, including three businessmen friends in Memphis, Tennessee. Despite threats on her own life, Wells continued her antilynching crusade through organizing, lecturing, and writing.

While my father fought relatively small battles against racism in Pasadena, African-American leaders across the country took the struggle to a new level. They waged battles in courts, in newspapers, and at street demonstrations. They supported educational and economic equity. Black leaders and activists such as Ida B. Wells, Booker T. Washington, and W. E. B. DuBois took different positions and offered different solutions to the problems of racial equality.

By the 1920s there were visible signs of hope and progress.

Black-owned and operated newspapers like the *Chicago Defender*, the *Pittsburgh Courier*, Boston's *The Guardian*, *Ebony* magazine (formerly known as the *Negro Digest*), the NAACP's monthly magazine, *The Crisis*, and the *Associated Negro Press*

Scholar and writer William Edward Burghardt DuBois (1868-1963) believed African Americans should be educated and activists. Du Bois was one of the founders of the Niagara Movement, the nation's first biracial civil rights organization, which later became the National Association for the Advancement of Colored People (NAACP).

Self-made millionaire Madame C. J. Walker (1867-1919) was an entrepreneur who amassed a fortune through her cosmetics business. Walker was an important supporter of the Harlem Renaissance.

Booker T. Washington (c. 1856-1915), a former slave, became a leading educator, author, and spokesperson for African Americans. He headed Tuskegee Institute in Alabama, an all-black college where students learned vocational skills. Washington believed this type of education would bring black people economic freedom, which would eventually lead to greater freedoms overall.

sprang up to tell the story of racial progress and encourage an antisegregation resistance movement.

There was also a small but growing professional class of African Americans who taught school, worked in hospitals as nurses and doctors, practiced law, and owned businesses. The Harlem Renaissance, named after New York City's vibrant black neighborhood, Harlem, brought forth great African-American writers, artists, and musicians. Artists like Jacob Lawrence; writers like Langston Hughes, Claude McKay, Countee Cullen, and Zora Neale Hurston; jazz musicians like Louis Armstrong and Duke Ellington; performers like singer-actor-activist Paul Robeson and dancer Bill "Bojangles" Robinson all rose to new heights of fame and popularity through the Harlem Renaissance.

Paul Robeson (1898-1976), an extraordinary singer, stage, and film actor, stunned audiences with his powerful performances in the film Showboat *(1936) and in stage productions of* Othello *(1930 and 1943). Robeson was later ostracized for his social activism.*

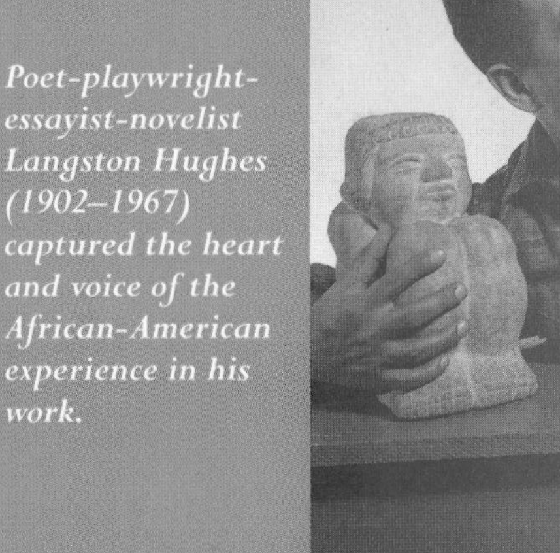

Poet-playwright-essayist-novelist Langston Hughes (1902–1967) captured the heart and voice of the African-American experience in his work.

Zora Neale Hurston (c. 1891–1960) was an anthropologist and novelist, best known for her book Their Eyes Were Watching God *(1937).*

Legendary bandleader Duke Ellington (c.)(1899-1974) took his famous jazz-swing orchestra all around the world.

My uncle Mack (l.), my father, and my grandmother Mallie at 121 Pepper Street, Pasadena.

Mack Robinson trains for the 1936 Olympics.

The glory of the Harlem Renaissance was short-lived. In 1929, it was replaced by a deep economic depression. Dad was in junior high at the time. He helped his family out by taking on odd jobs like delivering newspapers, cutting the neighbors' grass, and selling hot dogs during football games at Pasadena's Rose Bowl. And he endured the problems associated with being poor and fatherless.

When he was a teenager, Dad and his friends formed the Pepper Street gang. They didn't use drugs, drink alcohol, or start fights. But they did throw clumps of dirt at passing cars, swipe golf balls and sell them back to the golfers, and steal fruit from the local grocers.

Several key factors helped my dad avoid serious trouble. The first and most important was his devotion to his mother and the values she worked hard to instill in him. The second was his love of athletics. Most of Dad's energy went into playing sports. In 1935, he was a star high school football quarterback at Muir Tech, where he also played baseball, basketball, tennis, and held records in track.

Dad's older brothers were another big influence on him. He really looked up to Edgar, Frank, and Mack. Dad didn't always understand Edgar's odd behavior, but he admired his love of speed. Edgar's feats on roller skates and his bicycle were legendary. It was said Edgar could outrace the bus from Pasadena to Santa Monica, a 30-mile trip!

Frank was my dad's favorite brother, but Mack became his idol. When Dad was 13, he watched with pride as Mack won a place on the U.S. Olympic track-and-field team.

Mack went to Berlin, Germany, for the 1936 Olympic Games. Dad listened to all the track meets on the radio. The U.S. relay team, made up of African-American athletes Jesse Owens, Uncle Mack, Ralph Metcalfe, Johnny Woodruff, and Cornelius Johnson, won the gold medal. By the end of the Olympics,

Owens had won four gold medals. Mack had won a silver in the 200-meter dash.

The 1936 U.S. Olympic relay team's victory was more than a personal athletic triumph. The team won one for humanity. The performances of my uncle and other African-American athletes shattered Nazi leader Adolf Hitler's theory of racial superiority. The Nazis, who rose to power in Germany in the 1930s, believed that select white people known as Aryans were superior to all other races, including blacks and non-Aryan whites. German leader Hitler snubbed Jesse Owens by refusing to shake his hand at the Olympic medal awards ceremony, but black America and freedom-lovers everywhere celebrated this stunning victory over racism.

JOE LOUIS WINS

AT ALL STANDS ONLY 5c

Cleveland Call and Post

OHIO'S FASTEST GROWING WEEKLY

A ONE-ACT PLAY, 'BRAINS VS. BRAWN'

CHAMPION SCORES KO IN FIRST; AVENGES DEFEAT

Cleveland Goes Wild As News of Victory Flashes Over Radio

FLOORS SCHMELING THRICE TO ESTABLISH NEW RECORD FOR CHAMPIONSHIP DEFENSE

'$500 REWARD TO ANYONE WHO CAN PROVE I DON'T OWN THE CEDAR COUNTRY CLUB,' MASON

SCENES AT E.55TH AND CENTRAL -- FANS CELEBRATE LOUIS' VICTORY

Joe Louis's K.O. of Max Schmeling was headline news all over, as shown on this front page of a Cleveland, Ohio, newspaper.

The 1930s saw the rise of other African-American sports heroes. Joe Louis, "the Brown Bomber," was one of the most admired athletes of the time. On June 22, 1938, the heavyweight champion faced Germany's Max Schmeling in the ring. Like the 1936 Olympics, more than sports records were riding on the outcome.

Europe was on the verge of a second world war. Adolf Hitler gave Schmeling, his idea of the ideal "racially pure" man, a hero's send-off. Americans counted on Joe Louis to bring them victory. The fight of the century was on. It was as if war had already been declared. Louis knocked out Schmeling in two minutes, four seconds in round one. Joyous Americans all over the country—blacks and whites—celebrated in the streets.

But the victory party didn't last. The next morning, America woke up still separate and unequal.

A Determined Pair

After graduating from high school in 1937, Dad attended Pasadena Junior College (PJC), where he continued to build his sports legacy. Two important people came into his life at this point: a sprinter named Jack Gordon, and a young preacher by the name of the Reverend Karl Downs. Jack and my dad shared a love of sports and developed a close friendship that lasted a lifetime. The minister earned the respect of Dad and his friends. They soon learned that they could trust him with their problems. The Reverend Downs helped guide my father into manhood.

At PJC, my father set a national junior college record in track by beating his brother Mack's broad jump record. One newspaper called my father the greatest base runner ever to play on a junior college baseball team. That same newspaper named Dad athlete of the year. His exploits on the football field added to the legend. The Pasadena Elks gave Dad a gold football and named him Most Valuable Player. Needless to say, the college scholarship offers piled in. Dad chose to continue his education at the University of California at Los Angeles (UCLA).

The summer before Dad attended UCLA was a tough one. His mother moved into a smaller house, at 133 Pepper Street, leaving the house at 121 Pepper Street to her grown children. That same year, Dad's brother Frank was tragically killed in a motorcycle accident. In spite of the personal loss, Dad started at UCLA in the fall of 1939. He commuted by car from Pasadena to UCLA, where he once again lettered in four sports.

By senior year, he was named the best all-around athlete on the West Coast. He twice led the Pacific Coast Conference in basketball scoring, won the Pacific Coast Intercollegiate Golf Championship,

My father lettered in four sports at UCLA.

and reached the National Negro Tennis Tournament semifinals. But, perhaps the most significant thing to happen to Dad that year was meeting Rachel Annetta Isum . . . my mom.

My parents met on UCLA's campus in the fall of 1940. Mom was an eager freshman just thrilled to be in college. Dad was a mighty senior, stunning athlete, and "big man on campus." Mom was attracted to Dad immediately. She liked his warm, engaging smile, and the fact that he was confident without being cocky.

In the 1940s, black students at UCLA were a very small minority. Each day between classes they gathered in Kerckhoff Hall to eat and talk. This is where my mother and father met frequently and then began to date.

My parents were serious people with strong personal goals. Each wanted to be somebody. Mom wanted to be the first in her family to earn a college degree. Dad wanted to be a professional athlete.

As the romance between my parents heated up, so did America's preparation for World War II (1939–1945). As African Americans protested against their exclusion from the growing defense industry, Dad proposed to my mom. Not long after President Franklin Delano Roosevelt signed an executive order banning discrimination in all plants working on national defense contracts, my father was drafted into the United States Army. It was still segregated.

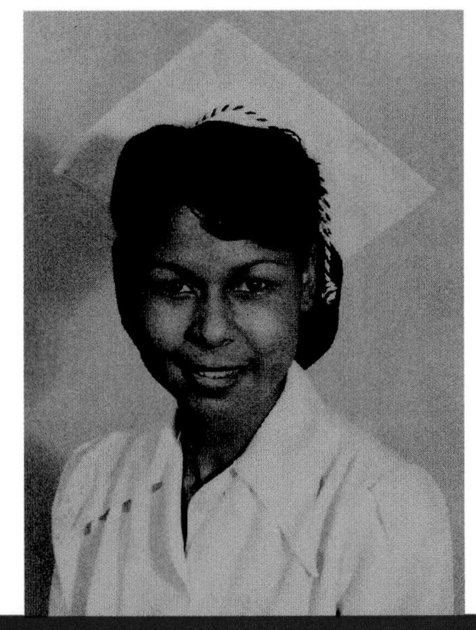

Mom studied nursing at UCLA while Dad served in the army. She graduated in 1945.

Dad's favorite sport in college was football.

Dad graduated from officer's training school as a second lieutenant.

In spite of the inequities in the armed forces, black soldiers served their country. In preparation for World War II, the U.S. government formed a training school for black pilots. The school was located at Tuskegee Institute in Alabama. The Tuskegee Airmen were the first African Americans to qualify as military pilots in any branch of the armed forces. By the end of World War II, almost 1,000 had won their wings at Tuskegee Army Airfield.

Dad was in the army for three years, from 1942 to 1945. Mom stayed at UCLA to get her degree. My parents were separated except for the times Dad came home on leave. My father wrote to Mom several times a week and sent a box of chocolates on Fridays. The separation was hard on both of them, but Mom believes that it helped prepare them for their life together.

Dad was stationed at Fort Riley, Kansas, and Fort Hood, Texas. Because of an old football injury, he wasn't sent overseas. Instead, he was assigned to the cavalry, where with the help of fellow soldier and boxing champion Joe Louis, he went to officers' training school and graduated as a second lieutenant.

The Tuskegee Airmen. More than a million black men and women served in the World War II armed forces. Many black entertainers joined tours of army camps. On the home front, black civilians worked in the war industries.

Neither Dad's rank of second lieutenant nor his college athletic celebrity protected him against the humiliation of serving in a segregated army in the Deep South. Dad served as a morale officer, yet could do nothing about the fact that the baseball team was segregated, whereas the football team was not. One way he protested this injustice was by refusing to play any sport for the army.

Toward the end of his stint in the armed forces, my father faced Jim Crow head on. During a bus ride from the army base into town, the bus driver ordered my father to the back of the bus, a section for black people only. Dad ignored the command; he knew his rights as a soldier. An argument followed, and Dad was arrested. Later, he had to defend himself in military court. The charges were dismissed.

On November 28, 1944, Dad was honorably discharged from the army. A year later, America and her allies declared victory over Hitler. With the war over, attention turned to peace at home.

August 15, 1945: U.S. Armed Service members in Paris, France, celebrate the end of World War II.

Dad was on leave from his army base. He and Mom announced their engagement at this dance.

1945: A Changing World

Satchel Paige (l.) and my father (r.) played in the Negro Leagues together.

After the army, Dad worked for a year as a coach at Huston-Tillotson College in Austin, Texas. He then played baseball in the Negro Leagues for one season (1945). That was the only league open to an African-American ballplayer at the time.

Between 1888 and 1947, black ballplayers were restricted to the Negro Leagues. The Negro Leaguers played a unique and exciting style of baseball that entertained millions in small towns and big cities across America. Negro League teams gave us great players such as Satchel Paige, Josh Gibson, Willie Mays, and Henry ("Hank") Aaron.

Despite the glory associated with Negro League baseball, it was still a part of a discriminatory system. Major League Baseball had an unwritten policy that kept nonwhite players out of organized baseball. Black ballplayers were denied the opportunity to play in the major leagues. Salaries were lower in the Negro Leagues, the schedules were less structured, and when the teams traveled south, they were forced to follow Jim Crow laws.

Because of its inequities, Dad questioned his future in professional baseball. Although my dad knew that the black press, some liberal sportswriters, and a few politicians were fighting for an end to Jim Crow baseball, he had little faith that it would happen in his lifetime. Little did Dad know that change was close . . . or that he was the prime candidate to break down the racial barrier.

The end of World War II signaled a turning point in America in many ways. Segregation was one area that was certain to change.

The black veterans returning from World War II were more determined than ever to abolish segregation. In 1948, President Harry S. Truman announced an end to segregation in the U.S. military. Other people were just as interested in desegregating civilian life. Some of them started with sports.

Because of its significance to American culture, baseball was the first team sport targeted for change. American baseball, which grew out of British ball-and-stick games like cricket and rounders, gained in popularity during the Civil War. By the end of the war, baseball was considered America's pastime. It seemed to represent all that was considered good about America: Democracy. Teamwork. Fair play. Excellence. It also represented America at its worst: Divided. Discriminatory. Unjust.

As a member of the Kansas City Monarchs, my dad played in 47 games hitting .387, with 14 doubles, 4 triples, and 5 home runs. His strong performance won him a slot as a shortstop on the Negro League All-Star team.

Determined to end institutionalized discrimination in baseball, sportswriters such as Wendell Smith of the *Pittsburgh Courier*, Frank A. Young of the *Chicago Defender*, Art Cohn from the *Oakland Tribune*, Sam Lacy of the *Baltimore Afro-Americans*, and Shirley Povich of the *Washington Post* wrote daily articles on the injustice of segregation within professional sports. They appealed to the Baseball Commissioner, to the owners of teams, to the ballplayers themselves, and to the fans who supported the game.

The questions these journalists raised went beyond the issue of

Baseball parks, like the game itself, were segregated.

race and into the economics of the game. They asked: Could baseball truly be considered America's pastime when black ballplayers and white ballplayers couldn't play on the same field? Could post-World War II teams afford to rebuild and be successful without including the enormous talent pool that existed within the Negro Leagues? Could the business of baseball grow when it was being accused of racism? Could the United States really consider itself a democracy if a portion of its population were denied basic human rights and opportunities simply because of the color of their skin?

1845
There are several myths about how and when professional baseball reached the continental United States. However, it is now commonly agreed that in 1845 the Knickerbocker Base Ball Club of New York adapted the European games of the past into the game we know today as baseball.

1846
The first recorded game is played on June 19 at Elysian Fields in Hoboken, New Jersey, where the New York Knickerbockers lost to the New York Baseball Club.

1869
The Cincinnati Red Stockings become the first openly salaried team and are considered the first professional team.

1876
The first major league, the National League, is formed in New York City.

1882
There are now two rival major baseball leagues in existence: the National League and the American Association. Neither league has any black players.

1884
Moses Fleetwood Walker from Ohio becomes the first black major leaguer when his team, the Toledo Blue Stockings, of the Northwestern League, joins the American Association.

1887
White players complain that they don't want to play alongside black players. Baseball owners vote not to offer any further major league contracts to black players.

1920
The first national all-black league is formed.

Branch Rickey fought for what he believed in.

With the country delicately balanced toward change and baseball under pressure to set the pace, someone within the executive ranks of baseball had to commit to breaking the color barrier. A couple of baseball owners had tried to be pioneers before 1945, but were unsuccessful. Then, with exquisite timing, Branch Rickey, president and general manager of the Brooklyn Dodgers, stepped forward. He was just the man for the job.

Wesley Branch Rickey was born December 20, 1881, in Stockdale, Ohio. He played baseball as a young boy in the Ohio countryside. Rickey attended Ohio Wesleyan University. Summers, he helped support himself by playing semipro baseball.

Even as a young man, Branch Rickey had strong values and firm beliefs. For example, while a student at Ohio Wesleyan, he began playing Major League Baseball for the Cincinnati Reds (1905). He refused to play games on Sundays because it was against his religious principles. Rickey was released from the team for taking this stand. From that point on, he had a clause written into all of his baseball contracts stating that he did not have to report to the ballpark on Sundays.

After Rickey graduated from Ohio Wesleyan, he went to law school, worked as an athletic director and baseball coach, and played big league ball for the St. Louis Browns (1906) and the New York Highlanders (1907). In his spare time, he lectured against legalizing alcohol. Rickey went on to manage the St. Louis Browns and Cardinals, the Brooklyn Dodgers, and the Pittsburgh Pirates.

In 1942, Branch Rickey was named president of the Brooklyn Dodgers. A year later, he went to the board members of the Dodger club and told them that he wanted to recruit players from Negro League teams. The board wasn't surprised. Rickey was well-known for bold moves. During World War II, he replaced seasoned ballplayers who were off fighting in Europe with boys as young as 15. In the 1930s, Rickey built baseball's farm system, which today is called the minor leagues.

When Rickey first proposed integrated baseball, the commissioner of baseball at the time, Judge Kenesaw Mountain Landis, was firmly against it. Landis died on November 24, 1944, and the new commissioner, A. B. (Happy) Chandler, took the opposite position and said, "I don't believe in barring Negroes from baseball just because they are Negroes." Branch Rickey agreed.

There were two basic reasons why Branch Rickey wanted to break baseball's color line. First, he deeply believed in equality and thought it was unfair to keep black ballplayers out of the major leagues. Second, he wanted to build the strongest team that would win games and excite the fans. Rickey knew that the talent pool in the Negro Leagues was too tempting for a smart businessman to ignore.

Branch Rickey took a year preparing to bring black ballplayers into the major leagues. He knew that success depended on finding the man who'd be right on and *off* the field.

Rickey studied the field using scouts to explore the pool of players. There were many Negro League players who were well-known and proven professional baseball players. Players such as Satchel Paige and Josh Gibson certainly headed the list provided by Mr. Rickey's scouts.

Branch Rickey studied the reports, listened to his scouts, and talked with black sportswriters. They universally agreed my father not only had the ability to play on a major league level, but was the right man to pioneer the integration of Major League Baseball.

Still, Rickey's decision was not an easy one. So what was it that really swayed him? What convinced him to take the risk with Jackie Robinson?

"I cannot face my God much longer knowing that His black creatures are held separate and distinct from His white creatures in the game that has given me all that I can call my own."

Dodger boss Rickey realized a lifelong ambition when he broke baseball's color line by signing Jackie Robinson (below). Behind Rickey is a picture of Abe Lincoln.

A Branch Grows in Brooklyn

Branch Rickey flourishes in Flatbush, champions the Negro in baseball, and is the father of major league's profitable farm system

By TIM COHANE

Jackie Robinson

Wesley Branch Rickey, 64-year-old president of the Brooklyn Dodgers, enjoys an indifferent press. Some sportswriters roar regularly for his head to be brought in on home plate, preferably with a baseball in his mouth as a gag in the literal sense. Others are less bloodthirsty.

"Branch has so got into the habit of quoting scripture," these latter point out, "that even when his motives are purely altruistic, his critics are still dubious."

Most Tongmen and Pollyannas alike, however, hailed Rickey in print or in private when he brought the Negro into modern organized baseball for the first time recently by signing Jackie Robinson, a shortstop, to a contract with the Dodgers' farm team at Montreal.

Nobody could reasonably suspect materialistic motives. Negro stars are not imperative to the pennant Rickey labors toward, nor could they improve attendance at Ebbets Field where a third-place team played to over a million paying fans last season.

In fact, signing Robinson may cost Rickey money, and Branch is about as allergic to money as he is to Rickey. Already, talent bird dogs have routed young prospects away from Brooklyn, because (Continued on page 72)

Look magazine, one of the leading magazines of its time, profiled Branch Rickey.

Why My Father?

On August 28, 1945, my father, who was playing baseball for the Negro Leagues' Kansas City Monarchs, met Branch Rickey to discuss playing for the Dodgers. There are many reports, but few eyewitnesses to this historic meeting, which took place at Branch Rickey's office in Brooklyn, New York.

Rickey knew all about my father's extraordinary athletic ability and that he'd successfully played on integrated teams in college. What he didn't know much about was what kind of person my dad was. So, before Rickey set up a face-to-face meeting, he called out to California to speak with people who knew my dad. He learned that Dad had been raised in a religious home by a mother whose values matched Rickey's own. He heard that Dad was a serious guy who didn't drink. He also heard that Dad was an aggressive competitor with a fiery temper. Rickey must have liked Dad's strong personality, but I'm sure he wondered how pressure would affect his playing. Nonetheless, he sent his scout, Clyde Sukeforth, out with instructions to bring Jackie Robinson to Brooklyn.

According to newspapers, magazines, books, and movies, Branch Rickey and my dad eyed each other cautiously during the warm-up discussion. Rickey launched into a series of questions that were less about baseball and more about character. "Did he have a girl?" the Dodgers' president wanted to know. Dad looked Rickey straight in the eye and explained that he was engaged and hoped to marry when he had a job.

Satisfied that my father would have a supportive partner, Rickey went on to talk about the need for my dad to hold back his anger, control his impulse to strike back, and play extraordinary ball in spite of fear. My father listened carefully. He felt excited, scared, and thrilled by the opportunity to play in the big leagues.

Rickey jumped into a monologue where he quickly shifted roles from that of a racist fan to a spiteful teammate. He taunted my dad with angry, mean insults.

My father leaned forward, hands fisted, feet planted firmly on the floor. I can only imagine the thoughts that must have run through his mind. This was more than just a chance to play in the majors. It was a chance to avenge the racism of his boyhood, to help right injustice.

Rickey was offering my father a terrific opportunity and tremendous responsibility. Dad was prepared athletically. He had the support of a loving woman and a steadfast mother. He'd matured over the years. He had his faith. But would he hold back his anger for the sake of the mission?

The role-playing ceased. My father eased back in his chair, unclenched his hands, and met Branch Rickey's steely gaze with confidence and determination. Rickey asked if he could stand the pressure. Would he control his temper against verbal and even physical attacks?

Dad didn't respond immediately. The same question was on his mind. He wasn't used to backing down when attacked.

Rickey made it clear to my father that the first three years would be critical. For the sake of racial equality, he'd have to adopt a nonviolent approach to change.

My father agreed.

Branch Rickey knew he'd chosen the right man. He knew that Dad had both the self-control and the courage to succeed. He and my father shook hands on a verbal agreement. "The Noble Experiment" began.

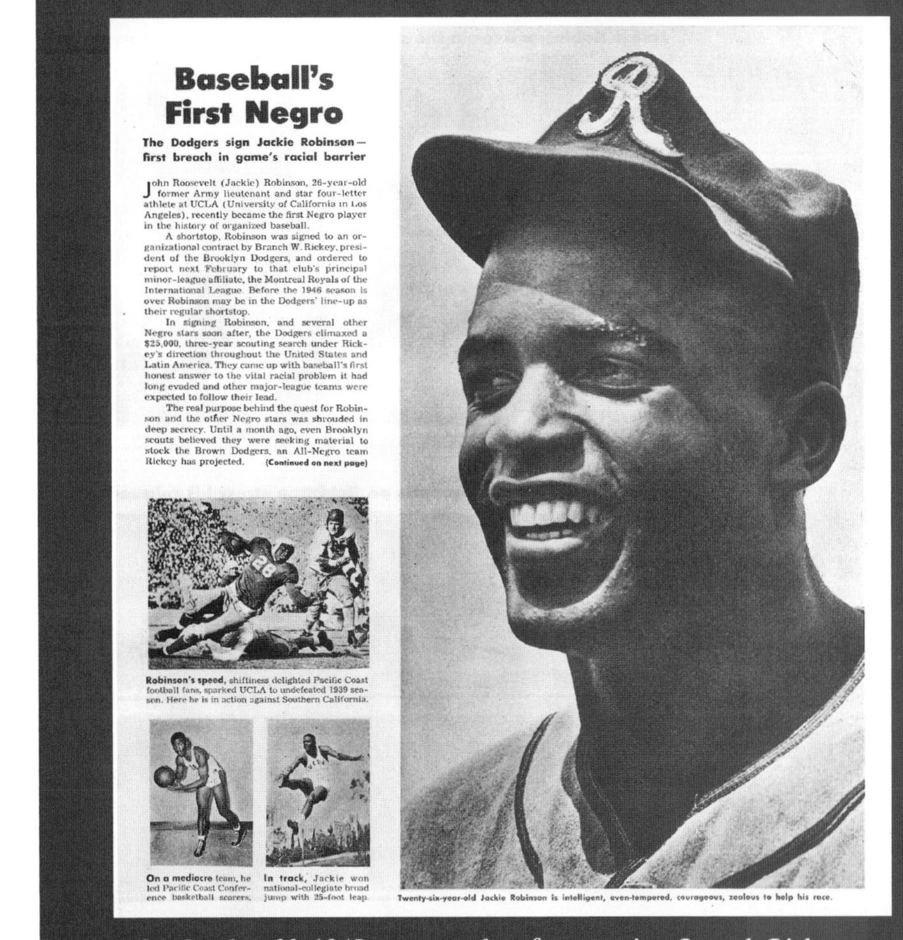

Baseball's First Negro

The Dodgers sign Jackie Robinson — first breach in game's racial barrier

John Roosevelt (Jackie) Robinson, 26-year-old former Army lieutenant and star four-letter athlete at UCLA (University of California in Los Angeles), recently became the first Negro player in the history of organized baseball.

A shortstop, Robinson was signed to an organizational contract by Branch W. Rickey, president of the Brooklyn Dodgers, and ordered to report next February to that club's principal minor-league affiliate, the Montreal Royals of the International League. Before the 1946 season is over Robinson may be in the Dodgers' line-up as their regular shortstop.

In signing Robinson, and several other Negro stars soon after, the Dodgers climaxed a $25,000, three-year scouting search under Rickey's direction throughout the United States and Latin America. They came up with baseball's first honest answer to the vital racial problem it had long evaded and other major-league teams were expected to follow their lead.

The real purpose behind the quest for Robinson and the other Negro stars was shrouded in deep secrecy. Until a month ago, even Brooklyn scouts believed they were seeking material to stock the Brown Dodgers, an All-Negro team Rickey has projected. (Continued on next page)

Robinson's speed, shiftiness delighted Pacific Coast football fans, sparked UCLA to undefeated 1939 season. Here he is in action against Southern California.

On a mediocre team, he led Pacific Coast Conference basketball scorers.

In track, Jackie won national-collegiate broad jump with 25-foot leap.

Twenty-six-year-old Jackie Robinson is intelligent, even-tempered, courageous, zealous to help his race.

On October 23, 1945, two months after meeting Branch Rickey, my father flew to Montreal to sign his contract with the Montreal Royals, the Dodgers' farm team, for a bonus of $3,500 and a salary of $600 a month. At a news conference, the Montreal Royals announced to the world that baseball's invisible color line had been broken.

The three-hour meeting between my dad (l.) and Branch Rickey (r.) is legendary.

Four months after Dad signed with the Montreal Royals, my parents got married. The Reverend Karl Downs performed the ceremony on February 10, 1946, at the Independent Church of Christ in Los Angeles. My mother's mother, Zellee Isum, was thrilled to plan the entire wedding right down to selecting Mom's china, silver, and crystal. It was wartime, so materials were hard to find. Still, Zellee insisted that my mother wear a satin dress. So, Mom went to Saks Fifth Avenue and found a prewar satin sample wedding dress that had a long train. Dad matched Mom's elegance in a sharp pair of formal wear as they pledged a lifetime of love and shared dreams.

My parents believed that marriage was the most important and fulfilling commitment that adults could make. Together, they reached for this ideal.

Eighteen days later, my parents began the long trek across the country so that Dad could report to the Royals' training camp in Daytona Beach, Florida. Branch Rickey had broken his own rule about not having wives at spring training and had invited my mother to join Dad.

When Dad and Mom arrived in New Orleans, they were forced to give up their seats on the plane. Then they were bumped from the next two flights. To add to the humiliation, they quickly discovered that because they were now in the heart of the South, they couldn't eat in the coffee shop. Luckily, Mallie, a southerner, had anticipated trouble and had packed my parents a lunch. Twelve hours later, Mom and Dad flew from New Orleans to Pensacola, where they took a segregated bus to Daytona Beach, Florida. It was a rough start . . . and shades of things to come.

Dad fields questions from reporter Wendell Smith (l.) during spring training.

My father joined black pitcher Johnny Wright and 200 white players for the Royals' practice. Eager newspaper reporters from New York, Pittsburgh, Baltimore, Montreal, and Brooklyn fired questions at the two black men. "What are you going to do if the pitchers start throwing at you?" "Duck," Dad joked. "Would you like to play for the Dodgers? Do you think you're good enough to play with Brooklyn now?" Dad answered confidently. He told the reporters that he'd played with white players before and was sure he'd make it through the minor leagues and on to the Brooklyn Dodgers team.

After practice, the white players went to the Mayfair Hotel. My parents, Johnny Wright, and black sportswriters Billy Rowe and Wendell Smith, were housed in the black community, either in a motel or a private home. They ate their meals in black restaurants. Through it all, Mom and Dad were inseparable.

Dad and Mom board a bus, heading for the Montreal Royals spring training in Daytona, Florida.

Netherland Plaza
Cincinnati

Darling,

The game starts at eight. I did so much want to meet you at the airport but time does not permit it. I love you so very much and knowing I am to see you tonight makes things a lot better. Harold will leave a ticket for you or you can sit with the people that met you at the airport. Incidently the way they knew you were [illegible] is Ernie called the

What I love about my parents' letters is that they always began with "Darling."

The day after they arrived, the Royals traveled south to Sanford, Florida for a week of spring training. As it turned out, Sanford was less welcoming than Daytona Beach. A few days into the training, Wendell Smith and Billy Rowe rushed my parents and Johnny Wright out of town because of threatened violence. Dejected, Dad said he wondered if the same thing would happen in the next town.

The Royals moved their practice back to Daytona Beach and had no further problems until they played games in Jacksonville and De Land, Florida. The Royals front office finally had to switch their remaining games back to Daytona Beach. During games, proud black fans crowded into the Jim Crow, or segregated, section of the stands while curious white fans filled in the remaining seats. On the field, the Royals' black players and white players worked as a team. When the game ended, they returned to their separate worlds.

After a successful spring training, the integrated Montreal Royals took to the field at Roosevelt Stadium in Jersey City, New Jersey, for the start of the 1946 season. Opening day was April 14, 1946. There were 35,000 excited fans in attendance. Because school was closed, there were a lot of kids in the stands. It was a clear, sunny, brisk day, more a football kind of day than baseball. Vendors sold coffee to help keep the crowd warm. The mood was electric as the mayor paraded on the field with celebrities and players for the singing of "The Star-Spangled Banner." Dad hit a home run in the third inning with two men on; singled three times; and stole two bases. Montreal won the game, 14 to 1. The fans mobbed Dad afterward, asking for autographs and wishing him well.

After the Jersey City opener, the Royals headed to Montreal, Canada. My parents were pleasantly surprised by the warmth and friendliness shown to them by the French Canadians.

Dad said he got a kick out of hearing the announcers at Montreal's stadium call his name out in French. He said it helped him escape the pressure of being Jackie Robinson. For that split second, he imagined himself to be just the new Montreal second baseman.

NOTE
WE HAVE ALREADY
GOT RID
OF SEVERAL
LIKE YOU
ONE WAS FOUND IN RIVER
JUST RECENTLY

Threatening letters were mailed to our home—but so were baskets of fan mail!

ROBINSON
WE ARE GOING
TO KILL YOU
IF YOU ATTEMPT
TO ENTER A
BALL GAME AT
CROSLEY FIELD
THE TRAVELERS

The Royals had different experiences in each city they played. Syracuse, New York, was worse than Sanford, Florida. During one game, while my father stood in the batter's box, a Syracuse player tossed a black cat toward him yelling, "Hey Jackie, there's your cousin clowning on the field." Years later, Dad told me he had been furious, but that he had responded by smacking the ball for a double. A few moments later a base hit sent him home with the winning run. As Dad rounded third base he shouted to the players on the Syracuse bench, "I guess that relative of mine is happy now, isn't he?"

In Baltimore, Maryland, the Royals learned there had been letters and calls threatening violence and a boycott if my father appeared on the field. The Montreal Royals played as scheduled. There were 3,415 people at the first game of the series. The small crowd was tense and angry. But as the Montreal and Baltimore series continued, the audience's mood changed. My father stole home during one game; the fans gave him a standing ovation.

Dad was big news when he got some big news himself: Mom announced she was pregnant. Dad was on the road, but Mom couldn't wait for him to come home. She called Dad, thrilled to report that they were going to have their first baby! Dad was so sure his firstborn would be a boy that he later wrote back a joyous letter adding that he would make his son proud of him.

Dad made good on that promise. During his one season with Montreal, he won the batting championship with a .349 average, scored 113 runs, ranked second in the league in stolen bases, and was voted Most Valuable Player in the International League. The Montreal Royals won the pennant and the Little League World Series. Today, the 1946 Royals are regarded as one of the greatest teams in the history of minor league baseball.

Despite the threats on his life and the weight of a people on his shoulders, Dad completed his first year with the Montreal Royals as a Most Valuable Player (MVP).

Mom holds my brother, Jackie Jr., while Dad shares in the parenting.

When he was on base, Dad studied the outfield. He knew exactly what had to happen in order for him to successfully steal a base.

Mom left Montreal in her eighth month of pregnancy to return to Los Angeles to await the birth of their first child. Dad joined her as soon as the season ended. True to his prediction they had a boy. Jack Roosevelt, Jr., was born November 18, 1946. He was a gorgeous baby with a head full of curly black hair.

Mom and Dad stayed on the West Coast surrounded by family and friends until Dad had to report for the Royals' spring training. Despite my father's successes in 1946, however, it looked as though yet another Major League Baseball season would start without a black player on any team's roster.

Then, on April 10, 1947, less than a week before the official opening of baseball season, the Brooklyn Dodgers played the Montreal Royals in the last game of the exhibition season. Dad hit into a double play in the sixth inning. Right after that play, a history-making announcement was made: The Brooklyn Dodgers had purchased my dad's contract from the Montreal Royals! Dad trotted back to the dugout. Fans and teammates cheered. Jackie Robinson was going to the majors . . . Jim Crow was going down!

Five days later, Dad played his first major league game at Ebbets Field, the Dodgers' stadium in Brooklyn, New York. An exuberant crowd watched the Dodgers beat the Boston Braves, 5-3. My father played first base and went hitless that game, but later that week belted out his first major league home run when the Dodgers played the New York Giants at the Polo Grounds.

Dad crosses home plate to score his first major league home run.

B
Dodgers
17
5

While Dad's teammates grew to appreciate his contribution to the team, they ignored him off the field. For the first couple of months with the Dodgers, Dad stayed to himself or with one of the black sportswriters. He said he felt the loneliness most when the team traveled. By June, however, things had changed. The team warmed up to my father. On train rides, they invited him to join in their card games. Eventually, Dad felt comfortable joking around with the other players.

Dad used to say that it didn't matter if somebody resents you. It only mattered if you could make him respect you. Two months into his first major league season, my father's skill gained him the respect of his teammates and the fans. That's my dad, number 42, with Dodgers captain Pee Wee Reese, number 1.

The BROOKLYN Dodgers
AFFILIATED CLUBS — SPRING TRAINING CAMP
DODGERTOWN, VERO BEACH, FLORIDA

My Darling,

I miss you very much and am glad when another day passes so I can be with you. I am sure you know how much I love you and that my love is stronger today than it ever has been. I know that it will continue to improve and we will have many more years of happiness ahead.

I guess by now you have had a chance to read about my weight and I am sure this year is going to be a real good one. I feel better than I have felt for some time and am working very hard to get into the best possible shape I can get into. To day made me feel very good as I was hitting well and moving better than I have for a long time. Its a matter of fact I believe I have a couple more years left barring accidents. We have been working pretty hard and I am sure everything will work out for the best. Bandy is a good ball player my dear but he'll have to sit on the bench and wait for an opening. I was very surprised to hit the ball so well today so I guess that as soon as I really get in shape I'll hit better. There really isn't anything more to write about. The newspapermen seem to sense my feelings as I have told them my only aim is to get into the best possible shape and let my work tell the rest. They stay clear of me and I am very happy for that. It makes my promise that much easier and even if it were hard I would be careful.

I love you Darling so much. Kiss the children for me and tell them how much I love them. Be sweet my Darling I know being away is tough but it only makes my love that much stronger. I keep wanting to hear your voice but keep fighting my self away from the phone. I love you and want to talk with you but am sure you understand.

Yours always
Jack

Here's how my mother remembered those early major league years: "During Jack's baseball career I attended every home game. I wanted to be with him and to experience his world. After games, I talked about how it felt to sit in the stands and hear fans yell at my husband. Jack talked about how hard it was to hold back his anger. Together, we fought off pessimism and despair.

"We worked hard to keep our fighting spirits alive and alert. We laughed and cried together. Most importantly, Jack was neither a victim nor a martyr as some have characterized him. We had many triumphs and victories to celebrate during his lifetime."

White fan reaction may have been mixed, but there was nothing ambiguous about the support from the Brooklyn fans and from African-American communities across the country. They loved my dad! Black families traveled long distances to go to ballparks to see him play. They gathered around radios at a neighbor's home to cheer Dad on. Sportswriter Sam Lacy once wrote: "No matter what the nature of the gathering, a horse race, a church meeting, a ball game, the universal question is: 'How'd Jackie make out today?'"

My parents and Jackie, Jr., settled into a small home in Brooklyn surrounded by a community that embraced them. There they met lifelong friends. As the baseball season progressed, Mom became friendly with a couple of the Dodgers' spouses, such as Gil Hodges's wife, Joan, and Pee Wee Reese's wife, Dottie.

Mom attended most of the Dodger home games. My brother, Jackie, Jr., went to many of those games with her.

About a month into the 1947 season, the Dodgers were in Cincinnati, Ohio, playing the Reds. The mood in the stadium was tense. Some of the fans started yelling at Dodger captain Pee Wee Reese, telling him that, as a southerner, he shouldn't be playing ball with a black man. Reese heard the shouting but refused to even glance in the direction of the stands. Instead, he walked over to my dad on first base. Reese put his hand on my father's shoulder and started talking to him. His words weren't important—in fact, afterward neither man remembered what was said. It was the gesture of comradeship and support that counted. As the two teammates stood talking, the fans got the message. They stopped heckling and settled down to watch the game. From that day forward, Pee Wee and my dad were friends, and they worked well together as teammates for many years.

Dad and Pee Wee Reese warm up with some stretches.

Dad gets hit by a pitch.

Major League Baseball players on other teams had mixed reactions to integration. Even late into the 1947 season, opposing players struck Dad with their cleats, or even pitched the ball at him, hoping to start a fight. Dad contained his anger. He glared at his aggressor until he had gathered the strength not to throw a punch.

The Brooklyn Dodgers won the pennant in 1947, but lost the World Series to the New York Yankees. By the end of Dad's first official year in the majors, his record spoke for itself. My father led the league in stolen bases and in sacrifice bunts, and was second in runs scored. He played in 151 of the 154 games that first season, all at first base, and brought a new aggressive style to the game. The *Sporting News* and the Baseball Writers' Association named Dad Outstanding Rookie of the Year in honor of his hitting, running, defensive play, and value to his team. He was the first winner of this award.

Dad accepts his 1947 Rookie of the Year award.

Dodger fans celebrate their team's 1947 pennant win.

During the off-season, a group of black New York City fans organized a "Jackie Robinson Day" at Ebbets Field. They presented my father with a new Cadillac, a television set, and other gifts. Dad's fame made him a popular guest on radio shows. In October 1947, he signed a contract for his autobiography that was to be written with Wendell Smith. That same year, a public opinion poll named my father the second most popular man in America. (Actor and singer Bing Crosby was the most popular.)

Two years into Dad's major league career, Mom found out that

My father's excellence on the field, his winning personality, and good looks made him one of the most photographed black personalities of the time. Sportswriters, black and white, covered his every move.

she was pregnant with me. She hoped for a girl. In anticipation of a growing family, my parents moved from Brooklyn to St. Albans, Queens. When I arrived on January 13, 1950, she and Dad were thrilled. My timing was impeccable. It was off-season for baseball and just before Dad had to go to Los Angeles for the filming of the motion picture *The Jackie Robinson Story*.

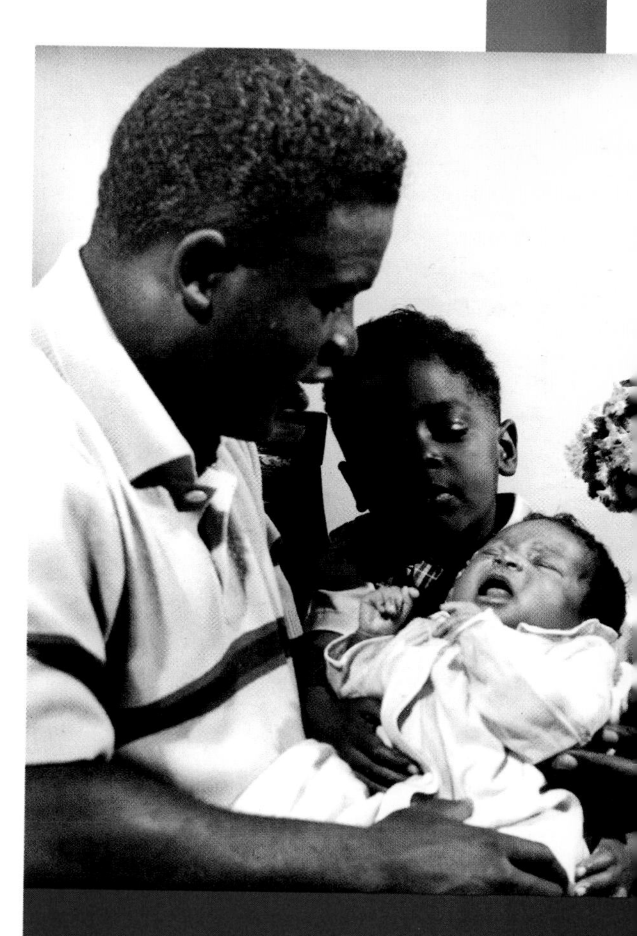

Dad, Jackie, Jr., and me

Kids with ten cents could find out all about my dad in this popular comic book, published in 1949.

That's me on the left, David in the middle, and Jackie, Jr., on the right.

Our family was complete two years later when my brother David was born on November 14, 1952. Luckily, Dad was in New York. He'd been at the hospital for the births of Jackie and me, and didn't plan to miss the birth of his third child, either. After the Dodgers lost to the Cardinals, Dad rushed from Ebbets Field to Doctor's Hospital in time for David's birth. Mom got sick and couldn't go home from the hospital with David. A family friend, Willette Bailey, came to stay with us at this point. She planned to stay until my mother was well, but ended up living with us until my brothers and I were out of the house.

Each March, we traveled with Mom to Florida for spring training and the exhibition games. Since Jim Crow laws were still in effect, we stayed at a motel in the black community while the other Dodger families stayed in a luxurious beach hotel across town. I was

Jackie Robinson

Dear Jackie, Sharon and David,

Mommy has been telling how what good children you have been and I am so glad to hear it. I will be coming home in a few days and for being so nice Mommy and I will take you to the circus to see the animals, clowns and all the thing that go with a circus. I am really proud of all of you and am alway telling people I have the best children in the world. I know you are going to be even better and you are going to work real hard to ha lot of friends like Mommy and Daddy ha

I know you are remembering you are to the house while I am away and are sho others what is right and wrong. Sharon is my big girl and mommy's helper. Its so nice having a girl so she can be the second mommy to look af the others be a big girl and help with David. I know David is growing and is talking a lot

so I hope he keeps it up.

I will be seeing you soon so be good children always.

Mom stayed at home with us when Dad traveled during the season. Even though he was very good at writing us letters and calling daily, we missed him. Keep in mind that this was before e-mail, nationally televised games, and 24-hour television sports stations.

too young to know the difference, but my parents resented being treated differently. Eventually, the Dodgers bought their own facility in Vero Beach, where black players and white players and their families stayed together.

With three growing children, Dad and Mom decided to build us a home in the country. In the fall of 1954, we moved from an integrated neighborhood in Queens, New York, where we lived across the street from Roy Campanella and his family. He was a fellow Dodger. We moved to an all-white community in Stamford, Connecticut.

By the time I was five, Dad had been playing with the Brooklyn Dodgers for 10 years. During that time, he'd helped the team reach the World Series six times. In 1949, he led the league in batting with a .342 average and received the National League's Most Valuable Player Award. From 1947 to 1953, Dad ranked fourth in the majors in batting average (.319), second in runs scored (773), and first in

My father's entrance into Major League Baseball opened up this world for other black players. The Cleveland Indians brought Larry Doby up a few months after Dad broke the color barrier. Don Newcombe, (c.) Roy Campanella, (r.) and Joe Black eventually became members of the Brooklyn Dodgers. The integration period within Major League Baseball ran from 1947 to 1956. The last team to bring a black player into their club was the Boston Red Sox.

stolen bases (166). Of his nearly 5,000 career at-bats, 51 percent were from the cleanup slot. The 1955 Brooklyn Dodgers had the best season. After yearly disappointments of losing the World Championship to the New York Yankees, the Dodgers and my dad won the World Series. "Wait till next year," their annual mantra, finally meant victory!

The 1955 Brooklyn Dodgers won the team's first and only World Championship.

A Civil Rights Champion

After the 1956 baseball season, it was clear that things had changed. Branch Rickey had left the Dodgers, and at age 37, Dad had passed his peak playing days. On December 13, 1956, the Brooklyn Dodgers announced that my father had been traded to their rival, the New York Giants.

Dad played along with the news of the trade, saying he'd give the Giants all that he had to give. The truth was, my father was aware that his baseball playing days were almost over. In anticipation of his retirement, he was investigating other opportunities. As the Dodgers announced the trade, my father stepped up his negotiations with a coffee manufacturer and restaurant chain, Chock Full O'Nuts, for a career outside of baseball.

I was the middle child between two brothers, David (l.) and Jackie (r.). This picture was taken for Look *magazine in 1956. We were four, six, and ten at the time.*

News of the trade sent baseball fans into an uproar. Angry letters poured into the Dodgers offices and into our home. The trade hit us hard, too. Dad had wanted to retire as a Brooklyn Dodger. He was angry that the team to which he'd been loyal hadn't even bothered to consult him on their plans to trade him. Without letting on that he intended to retire rather than accept the trade, Dad's agent made a deal with *Look* magazine. They got the exclusive rights to print my father's retirement story.

In the January 1957 issue of *Look*, Dad announced his retirement from baseball. The Giants tried to get my father to change his mind by offering him more money. Dad turned them down. He accepted a job with Chock Full O'Nuts in New York City.

At home, we celebrated the news. Major League Baseball players spend nine months of the year traveling and we knew that if Dad retired he'd be home with us more. So, as Dad prepared for life as a commuter, we imagined having him at home most nights in time for dinner. We liked the idea!

We were glad Dad wasn't going to be on the road so much and would be around for things like trips to the candy shop.

Dad's competitiveness was matched by our own when we challenged him to a game of Monopoly.

1957: Dad retires from baseball.

Dad exchanged his Dodgers' uniform for a corporate suit and tie in the winter of 1957. He became vice president of personnel for Chock Full O'Nuts. Like lots of other fathers in Stamford, Dad left home each morning at eight and returned most nights by six. Not being on the road meant he had time to give motivational speeches, write newspaper columns, raise money for civil rights organizations, join protest marches, speak to youth groups, play golf, and cut the lawn.

Dad also agreed to chair the National Association for the Advancement of Colored People Freedom Fund Drive. As NAACP chairman, he traveled around the country raising money for the nation's oldest civil rights organization. The first year of his tour, he helped raise more than $1 million.

Dad joined a group of investors and community activists to bring the first black-run bank to Harlem in New York City. They felt that a minority-owned and operated-bank was the only way to help rebuild Harlem's predominantly black community. On January 4, 1965, Freedom National Bank opened on 125th Street.

On special days, Dad took me with him to New York City. Our first stop was always his office at Chock Full O' Nuts.

My father helped raise money to support the sit-ins and demonstrations against segregation. He participated in voter registration drives, NAACP campaigns, gave speeches, and worked in politics.

July 23, 1962, my father is inducted into the Baseball Hall of Fame, which honors some of the sport's greatest players. My mother, as always, is by his side. Election to the Hall of Fame isn't a popularity contest, like the All-Star Game is now, where admission is determined by the fans. Players are voted into the Hall of Fame by the men and women who study baseball players and write about them. Negro League players, however, went unrecognized until Satchel Paige was inducted into the Hall in 1971.

On January 23, 1962, my father learned that he'd been elected into the Baseball Hall of Fame on the first round. He was happy and excited. There was a flurry of activity that led up to the July induction ceremonies in Cooperstown, New York. I was 12 at the time and not quite sure what all the hoopla was about. I asked my father what it meant to be chosen for the Hall of Fame. He said it was like being named to the Supreme Court if you were a lawyer. I got the point.

Dad's Hall of Fame induction was wonderful. Both of my grandmothers were there with us, along with Branch Rickey and

As children, our early experiences got us hooked on social activism. I will never forget the excitement of having Dr. Martin Luther King, Jr. (r.) visit our home for a fund-raising jazz concert for the civil rights movement. We also joined our parents in civil rights protest marches in Washington, D.C.

many others who had helped my parents throughout my dad's baseball career. Dad was the first African American inducted into the Hall. When he was presented with his plaque he spoke with such pride. I was so happy to be a part of this big day!

The following year, we hosted the first of many jazz concerts at our home to raise money for the civil rights movement. The 1963 concert was a fund-raiser for Dr. Martin Luther King, Jr.'s organization, the Southern Christian Leadership Committee (SCLC).

In addition to being a businessman, entrepreneur, and activist, Dad was a radio commentator for NBC and several local stations. He also wrote newspaper columns. Dad loved to talk and debate issues.

My father encouraged other athletes to lend a hand with the civil rights movement. Boxing champions Floyd Patterson (second from r.) and Archie Moore, along with baseball star Curt Flood joined him. Other professional athletes stayed away from the civil rights movement and politics. This troubled my father. He once asked, "Is there a medal anywhere which is worth a man's dignity?"

In 1964, my father left Chock Full O'Nuts to campaign for New York's Governor Nelson Rockefeller, who was running for president.

During the 1960s, Dad wore many different hats and faced many new challenges. The biggest challenge was his health. Shortly after he retired from baseball, Dad found out that he was diabetic. His health problems became more and more serious. Dad was only in his forties when he had his first heart attack; by his late forties, his diabetes had left him partially blind.

Still, the last seven years of my dad's life were filled with politics, business, family, friends, and golf. During that time, I married, and attended Howard University College of Nursing. My brother David completed high school at Mt. Hermon, Massachusetts, and went on to college at Stanford University. Mom taught nursing at Yale University. My older brother, Jackie, fought in Vietnam, received a Purple Heart, and then died tragically in a car accident when he was only twenty-four.

Mom, David, and I stood proudly beside Dad at the 1972 World Series. Dad's message was heard worldwide. My mom said, "Jack fought tirelessly for social justice and equality of opportunity for all people. He even ventured into hostile territory seeking to understand the complexity of issues dividing the United States. In doing so, there was always the risk f being rejected and misunderstood."

Despite our shock and pain over losing our beloved Jackie, we rallied as a family for what turned out to be our last year with Dad. That year was 1972. It was also the twenty-fifth anniversary of Dad's breaking the color barrier. In addition to special times together as a family, we celebrated Dad receiving a number of tributes. The final one took place on October 15, 1972. Dad threw out the first ceremonial pitch during the second game of the World Series in Cincinnati, Ohio. A record crowd was in attendance; an estimated 60 million people watched the ceremony on television.

All Major League Baseball teams were now fielding black, white, or Hispanic players, but the diversity stopped there. There were no nonwhite executives, managers or general managers in professional baseball. So, Dad felt it important that he use his last public address to remind us all that equality was an ongoing struggle. "I am extremely proud and pleased," Dad said in his World Series speech, "but I'm going to be more pleased and more proud when I look at that third-base coaching line one day and see a black face managing in baseball."

In addition to his many achievements in sports, my father was awarded the highest honors from civil and human rights organizations, religious groups, and the United States government. From the NAACP's Spingarn Medal to the nation's highest civilian award, the Presidential Medal of Freedom, my father's accomplishments on and off the field have been widely recognized.

Dad spent his entire life fighting for equality. He won some battles and lost others. He made some mistakes, but he also inspired millions. My father never lost hope or gave in to despair even when his health failed him. He once said, "A life is not important except for the impact it has on other lives." Dad lived his philosophy.

April 15, 1997. President Clinton (l.), my mother (c.) and Major League Baseball Commissioner Bud Selig (r.) celebrate the fiftieth anniversary of Dad breaking the color barrier.

My father helped change America. This lifetime of service continues to inspire.

Jackie Robinson's Legacy

We buried my father on October 29, 1972. In his eulogy, the Reverend Jesse L. Jackson reminded us that "no grave could hold this man down." More than 2,500 mourners watched as six former athletes, Boston Celtic star Bill Russell and Dodger teammates Don Newcombe, Joe Black, Junior Gilliam, Pee Wee Reese, and Ralph Branca, carried my father's silver-blue coffin draped in red roses out of New York City's Riverside Church. After the service, people lined the streets to pay their final respects as Dad's casket passed through Harlem on its way to the Cypress Hills Cemetery in Brooklyn.

A sign of mourning for my father

It was one of the saddest days of my life.

It took years for the pain and sense of loss to dull. But Dad would have expected us to stay in the game of life and to meet each challenge with strength and compassion. That's been my promise to him.

In 2002, my son Jesse helped pay tribute to my dad as part of Major League Baseball's Memorable Moments campaign. At the 73rd All-Star Game in Milwaukee, Wisconsin, my son reenacted my father's first moments as a major league player. Jesse, wearing a replica of my dad's famous number 42 Dodgers' uniform, stepped across first base, paused, hands resting on bent knees, eyes serious. At 24, he was five years younger than his grandfather had been when he broke baseball's color barrier. As the announcer played out the dramatization, he introduced my son to 43,000 cheering fans.

Mom and I sat proudly watching from the Baseball Commissioner's box as Jesse, who is two generations removed from the moment, accepted this profound yet brief connection to his grandfather. We'd raised my son with stories and pictures of my dad's achievement, but at the same time stressed the importance of defining life on your own terms. As we observed the confidence Jesse displayed that evening, we knew how far he'd come toward creating an identity separate and distinct from his grandfather.

And that's the challenge. It's taken me many years to understand and celebrate the fullness of my legacy. In achieving understanding, however, I've been both inspired and given a sense of direction that's enhanced who I am. At the same time, I've had the freedom to create a life of my own.

Jesse Robinson Simms at the All-Star Game.

New York Yankee Derek Jeter (l.) is one of the many players who have joined me (r.) in Breaking Barriers. *Through our work, we help children face obstacles in their lives.*

Each year, children across the United States select Jackie Robinson for their National History Day projects, and through their exploration of the man, they, too, adopt a piece of him into their lives. In Major League Baseball ballparks across the country, my father's number 42 is retired and proudly displayed along the outfield walls as a lifelong symbol of his legacy. Across the country there are organizations, programs, schools, parks, community centers, and other facilities that bear my father's name.

But perhaps our most significant family legacy is the Jackie Robinson Foundation. It was founded by Mom and several close friends in 1973, the year after Dad died. Through the Jackie

Bill Cosby (c.) is a major contributor to the Jackie Robinson Foundation. Here he poses for a photo with Foundation students and alumni.

Robinson Foundation, we strengthen young people by providing education and leadership development opportunities with the expectation that the path selected by each student will include giving back to their communities. More than 30 years after his death, Jackie Robinson Foundation scholars remain a living tribute to my father. Today, a thousand graduates of the program are in the world making significant contributions in the fields of their choice. Each graduate is unique and special. Each understands that family and career are only part of their work as an adult. They've all been trained that volunteerism is a lifelong commitment and that they must remain engaged and active in an ever changing world.

And so, the ranks of dedicated young leaders and followers committed to building a vibrant, productive, and richly diverse world are growing. The steps to forming such a society begins in childhood. It starts with making a promise to yourself, your family, and your community to be the best you can be so that when you're presented with the opportunity to lead, you'll be ready to assume your role.

Many years have passed since my father died. I still miss him terribly, but have found ways to continue to celebrate his life. Dad kept his promise to America. Yet the struggle for equality continues. It is my hope that future generations will embrace the challenges of a global society and find creative ways to challenge systems that are unjust.

My brother, David, lives most of the year in Tanzania, East Africa, but his coffee farming business brings him to New York several times a year. He is married and the father of eight, so we're blessed with a large contingent of Robinson children of varying ages, personalities, and offerings.

Mom, David, and I continue to pass on the lessons we've learned about life to all our children, those born into the family and those embraced by the family. Over time, we've seen this commitment bear fruit in many ways.

In 2001, Michael Jordan (l.) received our Robie Humanitarian Award.

Through their words and actions, my parents taught me the importance of keeping promises.